OUR MINI INFINITY

ARUN KUMAR | PRINCESS
SHIVANGI VERMA

It is with heavy hearts that we pay tribute to the memories of two remarkable men, Shri Rattan Singh, grandfather of Arun Kumar, and Dr. Sunil Kumar Verma, father of Princess Shivangi Verma. Both of these men have left an indelible mark on our hearts of those who knew and loved them, and their passing during the COVID-19 pandemic has left a void that will never truly be filled.

Shri Rattan Singh was a man of great wisdom and integrity. He was known for his kind and gentle spirit, and his unwavering commitment to his family and community. He was a source of guidance and inspiration to all those around him, and his passing has left a deep impact on all those who knew him.

Dr. Sunil Kumar Verma D.Phil (University of Oxford) was an accomplished Biologist, who was known for his passion and dedication to his field of study. He was a man of great intelligence and insight, and his contributions to the scientific community will be remembered for years to come. He was a loving father, and filled the void of a mother, friend and a guide as well. His loss, has left a deep wound in the hearts of those who loved him.

In honor of these two great men, we are publishing this book as a tribute to their memories. It is our hope that through these pages, their legacies will live on and continue to inspire future generations. We will always remember them and the love, guidance and knowledge they gave us. They will forever be missed.

Contents

Contents

Contents

Part 2

Preface

Preface to "Our Mini Infinity"

Welcome to "Our Mini Infinity", a collection of poems that will take you on a journey through the emotions and experiences of two teenage authors. This book is a testament to the power of the written word and the importance of self-expression. Through their poems, the authors invite you into their private world, a world that is full of hope, love, and self-discovery.

As teenagers, the authors found solace in writing down their thoughts and feelings. They used poetry as a way to process the emotions that came with growing up, emotions like love, pain, butterflies, confusion, loneliness, and joy. They found comfort in knowing that their words would never judge them and that they could always revisit their poems whenever they needed to.

What makes "Our Mini Infinity" unique is that it is written by two teenagers while all these emotions were at their peak. The authors' words are raw, honest, and full of heart, offering a window into the experiences and perspectives of two young people navigating the ups and downs of life. The poems in this book hold a backstory of their own, and every inch of it is a testament to the resilience and perseverance of the human spirit.

The world can be a busy and overwhelming place, and it can be easy to feel as though no one notices what we feel deep within. But in "Our Mini Infinity", the authors remind us that we all have our own personal worlds, our own "mini infinity" that we carry with us. And one day, we will find someone with whom we can share our infinity with, till the end of time.

We hope that this book will inspire and encourage you to find your own voice and to never stop expressing yourself through writing or any other form of self-expression. So, get ready to feel every emotion that you've ever experienced and to be transported to the world of "Our Mini Infinity".

Acknowledgements

Dear readers,

It is with the utmost gratitude and appreciation that we acknowledge all those who have helped to turn "Our Mini Infinity" into reality. This book would not have been possible without the unwavering support and encouragement of the following individuals and groups.

First and foremost, we would like to express our heartfelt thanks to Simmi Singh, who served as one of the most motivating mentors throughout this journey. Your guidance and support have been immeasurable, and we will always be grateful for your encouragement and wisdom.

Miss Umehani, you have been a constant source of support, always there to offer a listening ear and insightful advice. Your guidance has been invaluable, and we are so grateful for your friendship and support.

Tarun Kumar, your role as our technical and social media backbone was instrumental in the success of this book. Your creativity and tireless work behind the scenes have had a profound impact, and we cannot thank you enough for all that you have done.

Manvi Singh, your contributions as a motivating and ideal mate have helped shape this book into what it is today. Your support and guidance have been immeasurable, and we are so grateful to have you in our life.

Himanshu Dahiya, you have been one of the biggest cheerleading friends, always there to offer encouragement and support. Your unwavering belief in this project has been an inspiration, and we cannot thank you enough for all that you have done.

Of course, we cannot forget ourr parents, who have been our biggest supporters throughout this journey. Your love and encouragement have meant the world to us, and we are so grateful to have you in our life.

Finally, we would like to extend our sincere gratitude to our colleagues who have helped promote this book. Your support and enthusiasm have been inspiring.

Thank you all for your support, encouragement, and inspiration. It is because of you that this book exists, and we are so grateful for your help in bringing "Our Mini Infinity" to life.

With gratitude,

Arun Kumar & Princess Shivangi Verma

Life is a journey, with twists and turns

A path we must navigate, with lessons to learn

It's a rollercoaster ride, of ups and downs

But through it all, we wear our crowns

It's a tapestry, woven with threads of time

A kaleidoscope of experiences, that make us shine

It's a symphony, of joy and pain

A beautiful melody, that we all play

Life is a gift, to be cherished and held dear

It's a precious moment, that should never be feared

It's a chance to grow, to love and to live

To make a difference, and to truly give

Life is a journey, with no certain end

But in the moments that make up life, we'll find our friends,

So hold on tight, and enjoy the ride.

1. " I MISS US "

As a boy, I stood tall,
By my grandfather's side, through it all.
But now he's gone, and I'm left to grieve,
My heart broken, and my spirit cleaved.
I was by his side, till his very end,
But even though I didn't cry, I felt it all, my heart rend.
I held back my tears, and kept my head high,
But inside, I was broken, into a thousand pieces, and I
couldn't help but sigh.
I miss the way he used to tell his stories,
The way he used to make my worries and fears, all
disappear.
I miss the way he used to hold my hand,
And the way he used to make me understand.
But even though he's gone, I'll never forget,
All the things he taught me, and the love he kept.
I'll carry on his legacy, and keep his name bright,
And I'll always remember him, with love and light.
-Arun

2. MOONRISE

Have you ever seen a sunrise?
So beautiful and refreshing..
Filled with energy of a new day!
It's sunrays so encouraging...
While i hear everyone talk..
About the pretty sunrise..
I cannot help but wonder..
About the silent moon in the sky..
Have you ever heard..
About a "Moonrise"?
That how peaceful it is..
It makes the sorrows surmise..
The moon rises...
As the bright sun overshadows..
But it stays calm,
Waiting, waiting and waiting...
It waits for the sun to sleep,
Sad souls wait to weep..
In the moonlight no one would see..
Yet, the moon spreads the glee...
The moon is love in pain...
It's a slow song playing in rain...

Moon smiles and says to sad souls..
That it's okay, to loose and gain...
What if the sun never slept?
What if moon never showed up?
Where would've we hidden our tears?
And secrets deep withing that we kept..?
The dreamy moon and it's moonlight,
Show us how to shine in the night..
It give us calm, peace and quiet..
It help us through our black and whites..
How would dreams come true?
If you never even saw one?
It would be like aiming in the dark,
Walking without any destination!
The dreams we see in this time..
Starry nights makes me feel fine..
The moment you share with yourself..
Wouldn't have happened, without moons help..
The sun is hardwork,
The moon is patience..
The sun says never give up..
But in the moon we sink in..!
Life can be so rough,
You can't stay strong forever!
Feel the breeze brush against you,
And let the broken self recover..

Oo dear moon,
May you rise,
and make our sorrows surmise..
after every day,
We need you to show us the way..
I know no one ever says..
But my nights,
Are better than my days!!
-Princess Shivangi Verma

3. " AUGUST WRITES "

Sometimes I sit and get lost thinking about that day,
god sent me an angel,
I thank him for not taking you away.
with a blink on an eye you changed my world,
I still cannot believe, that you are really my girl.
you are really a best friend who will always be there,
you are someone, who really cares.
you don't know what you have done for me,
you've turned me, to the best I can be.
you're an angel sent from above,
to take care, and show me what is love.
now I have found what I never thought for,
I have found that, it's your love and nothing more.

you made my unnecessary sadness a thing of past,
because you have showed, a the love that will last.
when I was in the darkness, you showed me the light,
I wish I could be there and hug you soo tight.
my love for you will always remain in my heart,
and I know that nothing can really tear us apart.

trust me , you will always be my mine,
and my love for you will remain by the end of time.
I wish I will always talk to you till the end of day,
but now I am running out of words to say.
so I'll end this by a line you already know,
I love you more than I can ever show!
-Arun

4. WITH YOU

Walking down the memory lane,
Thinking about the good times,
thinking you could be mine,
thinking about your faint smile.
I don't want to say it cause I am afraid,
I don't want to tell it cause I am so scared,
I don't want to break your heart,
Again and again.
Making new memories of these times,
looking in your eyes with a little smile,
but don't want to fake it all,
My love for you will never get small.
I don't want to tear up your eyes,
I don't want to be the harsh sunshine,
I just want to love you like your mine,
I hope It doesn't sound like a crime.
Fill up your life with all the rainbows,
walking on the path that I chose,
I still care about you much more,
I hope your heart is open as if it was a door.
Make the rain pour from the heights,
dancing like a bird beneath the blue sky,

make you smile once in a while,
Sit with you and our short life.
Spend all my time with you and be alive,
share my feelings with you, laugh and cry,
Make your day and laugh along,
Oh my dear i Love you a lot.
- princess shivangi verma

5. "YOU ARE THE REASON"

You are the sun that brightens up my day,
The north star that guides me on my way.
You are my refuge in times of strife,
The beating heart of my very life.
Your smile lights up my darkest hours,
And in your arms I find the power
To rise above the pain and strife,
And live a life of joy and light.
You are the wind that lifts me high,
The gentle rain that brings life to the sky.
You are the light that shines within,
The fire that warms me from within.
You are the teacher of love and care,
The one who's always there.
You bring out the best in me,
And set my heart and soul free.
You teach me how to love and give
How to live and how to forgive
In you, I find my soul's true mate
A love that's strong and never late

With you beside me, I am strong,
My journey through life is a beautiful song.
For you are the reason, the reason I live,
The reason I love, and the reason I give.
-Arun

6. FOREVER AND EVER?

"FOREVER AND EVER?"
I've been so hurt..
That i don't want to try anymore..
Everything i ever wanted..
Either I never got it..
Or I lost it..
And I'm still loosing..
More and more everyday..
Even when I try and pull myself up..
Something pulls me down..
Deeper into the void..
It's about me..
It's about my life..
About what i could have done..
To make it right..
And i didn't...
I kept walking into it..
And now I'm so deep and lost..
i don't know the way back..
I need love and care...

And a someone with whom I could share..
All the feelings that i feel..
All the secrets I live with..
They are too heavy now..
I can't take it anymore...
I can't take life anymore...
Oh, how I long for the old times...
But it's long gone...
And it will return never...
Will i stay miserable?
Forever and ever?

-Princess Shivangi Verma

7. "I DON'T THINK SHE KNOWS "

my feelings are getting deep
they are taking big, a long leap
going from friend to crush
what a rush ,
I love how she looks and who she is
how calmly she makes me feel this.
She is beautiful and smart with a strong heart
For Now we are friends , nothing can took us apart
and I don't think she knows

her beautiful eyes are really like stars
they are so deep and bright ,can't find scars
they pour emotions in the ragging rivers
they made me believe that Santa always delivers
when she talks I can't help but watch her lips
to notice their shape and curves when they dip
wait ,why am I looking? I don't even know.
I can't help but wonder if she even knows.
Still she hasn't got a clue.

Now school is at an end at 12 noon.
I wonder if she cares that I'm moving soon
we are parting that day after school for many months.
I just wish I could have kissed her just once.

Now that I have said it with my poetic skill
I don't think she knew, and now she never will.
-Arun

8. DEEP OCEAN LOVE

Deep ocean love,
I feel the water above,
I'm drowning in this even more,
I'm not what i was before,
Trusted someone with closed eyes,
Silly me couldn't see the lies,
Once we were in it neck deep,
They left me there alone to weep,
They forgot couldn't care less,
Over these traitors i used to obsess,
I'm trying to breathe but it's getting hard,
I look around all i see is dark,
I wonder if I'll ever get peace,
I wonder will this pain increase,
Loved him when he was a shining star,
Loved him when he fell apart,
Loved so deep i can't come back,
Loved so pure now love i lack,

All you returned was rose of thorns,
And I thought that you made me yours,
Told pretty lies and made me believe,
Now I'm a single leaf on an old tree...
I wonder if all are the same,
I see betrayal in every name,
I lost myself in the deep ocean love,
My eyes close as i feel the water above.
-princess shivangi verma

9. " WE ARE LIKE STARS "

We are like stars, shining bright,
Bursting open with all our might.
In moments of doubt and fear,
We think that death is near.
But in truth, a transformation starts,
As we turn into supernovas' art.
Radiant, fierce, and full of grace,
Our true beauty shines in space.
So when we look at ourselves again,
We see the beauty that remains.
Brighter than before, and bolder too,
Our light shines on, shining true.
So let us embrace this change within,
And know that beauty can begin,
When we burst open, with a might,
Like stars shining, in the night.
-Arun

10. DREAMS OF THE DEAD HEART

The end seems so tragic..
I don't know where to start..
The warmth of this sinful magic..
And dreams of the dead heart...
Blooming hearts seem so pretty..
Don't you crave for one too?
All of it seems so giddy,
Ask the one who has seen it through..
Stars scream at the shining sky..
Don't believe this shining lie..
One day the love will pacify..
Even if you want to keep it alive...
Blooming hearts wither away,
What remains is not the same,
He left who said would stay,
Who should I now give the blame?
Dead hearts dream of love,
Love that comes from above,
It begs for it, it cries, it strives,
Love is dead now, but it still tries...

Making of every heart is alike,
Every heart breaks and mends,
Sad soul subsides the strike,
Outer self is happy it pretends.
Dead dreams of the dead heart,
Dead love never returns,
The end is not how it starts,
Every shining star shines and burns
-Princess Shivangi Verma

11. " IT'S ABOUT YOU "

Brave and beautiful,
not a flower or a tree
much prettier then them,
only smarty can see.
loving and caring,
right down to the deepest point of my heart.
filling me with happiness
and much more.
eyes are so sparkling,
smarty can't look away.
gorgeous and shining,
all through the day
here in your arms
is where i belong,
the beating of your heart is like
a beautiful song.
-Arun

12. HEARTS OF STONE

HEARTS OF STONE
I was a home with an open door,
You walked in and i let you,
I did all that, what for?
I thought it would be us two.
I made you mine deep inside,
I made all your blue's bright,
But also deep down i cried,
You were never mine as much tried.
You stayed but then,
you found another,
I really cared but,
You did not even bother.
You wanted to go now,
And i couldn't stop you
You walked out,
It was slowly all coming true.
Eyes filled, door open,
Lips sown, heart broken,
You kept walking, never looked behind,

They said another i will find.
But i couldn't let this happen once more,
Closed my eyes and sat on the floor,
Can't let them hurt me like before,
From now i will lock the door.
-Princess Shivangi Verma

13. "HOPE YOU WILL NOTICE"

what should I do to make you, to notice me?
Change my hairs , the way I talk?
My clothes, the way I walk?

We know each other for some time now,
but still I am invisible to you.
In your script, I'm just a friend
Nothing more, nothing less.

I settle for friendship in the end
Because now I don't want a mess.
How deep my feelings run
When I see you smile, everyone makes my fun
Whenever I see your face, I close my eyes.

In my script , you are same in all the dyes.
But now, I'll keep my secret to myself
And take everything back in the corner of my shelf.
Till the day you finally see
That how you and I were meant to be.

I'll wait for you but can't do it for too long
Because sooner or later I'll be gone.
I hope you'll notice me.
-Arun

14. AWFUL LOVER

Everytime I feel i crossed it,
Something pulls me back,
I remember all the crying,
How it ended in a snap.
You called it all a joke,
How dare you forget the time,
You were the reason I broke,
Never asked if i was fine.
I want to just forget it,
Everything that we had,
Just like how you did,
Never even felt sad.
Broke me, her and now another,
Do you ever feel what i do?
You were just an awful lover,
I hope you get one yourself too.
-princess shivangi verma

15. " THE MAN "

There once was a man so brave and bold,
Who had feelings for his best friend of old.
He wanted to confess his love, knew it would be tough,
For the girl he loved already had someone else.
His heart was broken yet he kept strong willed,
Knowing that if he confessed things might get killed.
So in the end with heavy heart and sighs galore,
He squashed those feelings down even more.
He loved her with a passion bright,
A flame that burned within his heart,
But though he gave all of himself,
she seemed immune to its spark.
Though in both joy and pain they shared their days
together,
She could not return the feelings that he held so deep
inside.
Unable to express what he was feeling or what it meant for
him to try;
The love which filled his soul refused to die.
-Arun

16. YOUR LIES, OUR TIES

Remember the days we planned our future?

When we spoke of love so pure?

By the lake, our bond would nurture,

But the dream of us, we did demure.

You whispered words so sweet and fair,

Of a love that would always repair,

In your arms, I found my safe lair,

But now, I'm shattered beyond repair.

"Forever and always, my perfect one,"

Such promises, now, all gone,

My love for you, so bright, so strong,

Now, in my heart, only emptiness belongs.

"No one could love me more than you,"

Words that now seem false, it's true.

My love grew everyday for you,

But now my heart aches, what did I do?

The bond we shared, a love so rare,

But you ran away, without a care.

Left me with tears and endless pain to bear,

Do you even feel the hurt, the unfair?

You never cared for my shattered soul,
Only speaking when you had to,
My anger now, continues to grow,
I regret, the day, I said "I love you."
-Princess Shivangi Verma

17. " THESE SIMPLE RHYMES "

When you smile, you makes me smile
when you laugh, you makes me laugh.
Your eyes are enchanting
you make my thoughts seem daft .

since the day I first saw you
Feelings for you,the way they grew.
That first conversation,my heart lagged
and those butterflies flipped and flapped.

The way I spill these simple rhymes,
my mind think of you over time and time.
why don't you ask me to dance
on those slow songs of endless romance?
I hope this doesn't feel creepy
please don't mind my thoughts have flown freely.
Just you know that what I speak is really true
And I have fallen this deeply just for you.
-Arun

18. REMEMBER ME

Somewhere in my mind,
i still care,
My love is blind,
I have feelings to share.
Its been quiet a while,
We haven't talked,
In my heart there is a missile,
With you i want to walk.
The pain i feel now,
will vanish tomorrow,
You tell me how..,
Your love can i borrow?
Please don't go,
I will miss you,
My hopes are low,
My worries grew..
Let me see you one last time..,
It's for your own good,
I know you will be fine,
Remember me if you could...
-Princess Shivangi Verma

19. "RAIN"

He stands alone in the rain,
With heartache and pain.
His friend has gone astray,
Leaving him on this lonely way.
His future once shone so bright,
Now shadows cast a darkened sight.
He thinks of what tomorrow will bring,
But all he does is sadly sing.
The rain beats down with such force,
His sadness spills with no remorse.
His 20s were meant to be carefree,
But now they feel like a blur to see.
He hoped life would turn out grand,
But instead it's filled with reprimand.
Still, he stands there in the rain,
With courage and hope to gain.
For though his friend is gone today,
The memories they made will never stray.
And though life may not go as planned,
His spirit remains steadfast, unbranned.
-Arun

20. A BROKEN HEART

Baby you freaked out when i said that i loved you..

But what about me?

Should i break myself for your new start?
Do you even love me?
Take my love and fix your past?
You gave me no closure,

left and said it's not my fault?
Did not try to ask me how i was,
you could have atleast called!!
Everyday i regret those moments,

i gave you love and time,
You took it all for granted,
and the world calls my love a crime.
If i had a watch, that would take me back and stop it all,

I would forget you forever, and i wouldn't hesitate at all!

I gave you love, you made promises in return,
Turns out you didn't mean them,
in hell those promises burn!

I hope i never see you again,
i hope you feel the way i felt,
But if i do..I'll ask you just once...
why couldn't my love make you melt..?
-Princess Shivangi Verma

21. " THE ACHE "

Pictures, frozen moments in time,
Reminders of when you were mine.
Your shining eyes, your gentle smile,
Each morning, I'm alone, in denial.

The ache within me, a constant blaze,
A love for you that time cannot erase.
I miss you so much, it's hard to bear,
A pain that never fades, I just want you here.

People say time will heal the wound,
But I'm not ready, I want you around.
So I hold onto these pictures, with care,
Memories of you, forever fair.

In my heart, you will always stay,
A love for you, that will never fade away.
These pictures, frozen fragments of time,
Will always remind me, of when you were mine.
-Arun

22. BUTTERFLIES

Butterflies
Butterflies in my head,
I see our future ahead,
A path that love has led,
It's just like how you said.
Making our bond stronger,
I want it to last longer,
We'll Walk along together,
And make it last forever.
I love the way you smile,
I think of you every while,
You make my heart fly,
With you i feel so high.
Can you please hold me tight?
Please never go out of sight,
Your sunshine in the dark night,
With you it all feels so right!
-Princess Shivangi Verma

23. " MOVE ON "

A young man, with a heart of gold
Watches as his love, is given away, old
He sees her walk down the aisle
With another, to exchange a smile
He watches as they exchange rings
His heart breaks, as the church bells sing
He sees the love in her eyes, so true
But it's not for him, and he knew
He stands alone, as they say their vows
His heart aches, as he bows
He wants to leave, to escape this pain
But he can't, it's all in vain
Tears stream down his face
As he sees his love, in another's embrace
He knows he must let her go
And with a heavy heart, he takes it slow
He turns and leaves, the hall in silence
His heart broken, in this love's reliance
He knows the road ahead will be long
But he'll keep moving on.
-Arun

24. EARTH'S INNER DESIRE

"EARTH'S INNER DESIRE"
Earth's Inner Desire
Earth says to the sky above,
She asks him about their love.
Although her love is pure,
She always feels so insecure!
She's still, the air is moving..
Birds sing and trees grooving...
The sky shows her day and night,
The earth depends on his light..
Her still soul ignites a fire of desire,
She always wishes to rise higher.
Her close to the beautiful sky,
The misery - "she cannot fly".
Clouds rain extinguishing her thirst,
In him she is now immersed..
The never meet, the distance has no end,
But somewhere far away, we see them blend.
-Princess Shivangi Verma

25. " BE MY HEART "

Did you see the rainy moon,
So bright against the night?
It shone like a beacon,
Guiding me to you in sight.

I long to be by your side,
To bask in love's sweet bliss,
And hold you close beneath the sky,
In the embrace of a lover's kiss.

But I fear I stand alone,
My love for you unreturned,
A one-sided flame that's grown,
Burning bright, but never earned.

And still, I hope and pray,
That one day you'll see,
The love that I hold inside,
And come to share it with me.

So let us run through the meadows,
Where the moonlight dapples and shines,

And let us lay down our swords,
And never take fight to our bed.

And if I should fall from this world,
Please hold me in your heart,
For even in death, my love for you,
Will always be a work of art.
-Arun

26. HIDDEN THOUGHTS

Our eternal soul,
Agony hidden in it,
These feelings are explicit,
A path we cannot quit.
The air blends...
In my burning thoughts,
Thoughts only i know about,
Thoughts that are getting loud!
Your touch is so tender,
It makes me glow..
My vision is now blurry
And i let the thoughts flow...
I'm looking for an end..
But i don't want it to stop!
Don't know how to repent,
I think I might be lost..
-Princess Shivangi Verma

27. " IN THE RAIN "

In the rain he stands, alone and forlorn
Heartbroken, borked up, and so very torn
Watching her walk away, with another by her side
Leaving him standing there, to suffer and abide
As the rain pours down, drenching him to the bone
His tears mix with the drops, as he's left all alone
Memories of her flooding back, like the stormy weather
He wishes for her return, now and forever
But she's gone, and he's left with nothing but pain
As he watches the love of his life, disappear in the rain
He knows he must move on, but it's hard to do
When the love of your life, is no longer true
The rain continues to fall, as he makes his way home
His heart heavy with loss, and feelings unknown
But he knows that time will heal, and love will come again
And for now, he'll weather this storm, until the end.
-Arun

28. SOMEONE

I dream of finding someone,
Someone who really cares..
I keep trying to make them mine,
But the paper of dream tears...
You look into my eyes deep and true..
You promise me you'll stay how you do...
My eyes fill with hope and i trust once more,
They leave forgetting the all the love we wore...
I break inside my hopes fall deep down..
Love has now turned me into a stupid clown...
Is it just me or is this how it is done..?
I sit and wonder...if I'll ever find that someone...
-Princess Shivangi Verma

29. " OLD SCHOOL "

A young man on a journey,
To find a school that would be
The perfect fit for his dreams
And make his future bright it seems
But as he walked the streets alone
He met a stranger, a girl unknown
Their eyes met, and they began to talk
Sharing stories, taking a leisurely walk
They laughed and talked for hours on end
And soon they knew, they'd be friends
With time, they found they were more
Perfect for each other, forever to adore
They traveled the world, hand in hand
Helping each other, to grow and expand
Through struggles and hardships, they stood
Together, forever, they knew they would
And when the time was right, they wed
With love in their hearts, they said
I do, and promised forever
To be each other's treasure
Now they look back on that day
When they met as strangers and they say

That it was fate that brought them together
And they'll be forever in love, forever.
-Arun

• 46 •

30. A CIGARETTE

It's normal!! Everybody does it!!
You should do it too!! It's fun!!
It seemed fun i admit...
A desire in me had begun...
But i shouldn't..it's wrong...
Come on just this one time..
It won't take so long..
And it's not a crime!!!
I saw them puff in and puff out..
They seemed so relaxed and at peace..
I thought of it throughout...
As all their worries decreased...
I wanted to do it too..
But..deep down I knew...
It was happiness for a few...
After its gone, its will be blue...
I refused...
i knew it was right..
They called me a coward...
But i remained quiet...
It's not the right time..
To explore these ways..

Even though it's not a crime...
It won't pass like a phase...
I'll do it when I'm ready..
when i know i can handle me...
I won't get blinded by its glee...
The day I'll oversee...
-Princess Shivangi Verma

31. " ONE DAY "

An old man sits and ponders
His life, once full of wonder
Rain patters on the window pane
As memories flood his brain
His hands, they gently shake
As he sips his tea, to warm and make
Thoughts of his dear wife
Who helped him through life
He remembers how she stood by his side
Through the joys and the tears that have dried
She helped him to grow and to thrive
With her love, he felt truly alive
As he sits, lost in thought
He feels a gentle hand that he's caught
His wife, she rubs his hand
And plants a kiss on his forehead, so grand
With her touch, his heart is filled
With memories of a life that was distilled
Into moments of love and of grace
In this quiet and peaceful place.
-Arun

32. A KISS?

I saw you kiss her..
You seemed so lost..
You showed me the picture..
My hearts in a frost..
I got some feelings..
But you don't really care...
Why would you kiss me?
Your hands in her hair...
She is picture perfect..
Perfect in real life...
I am a puppet..
Filled head with lies...
Why would you do this..
I wanna ask...
She got the first kiss...
Will I get the last?
-Princess Shivangi Verma

33. "JOURNEY"

As we journey through life's many twists and turns,
Memories linger, the good and the burns.
Friends we've made, now seem so far away,
Leaving us feeling lost, every day.
But don't despair, hold your head up high,
For these phantoms will soon pass by.
Days of joy, will return once again,
And with them, a new life to begin.
Life is ever changing, it's true,
But with each new chapter, there's a breakthrough.
So hold on tight, and don't let go,
For the journey ahead, will surely show.
You are stronger than you know,
And the future ahead, will surely glow.
So embrace each moment, with a smile,
For life's many phases, are all worth the while
-Arun

34. LOST

The only chance i had ...
I lost it to my confidence...
The only part where I went wrong...
I don't know where it is...
What could i have done differently?
Was this supposed to happen?
Is this end of my good time?
Why... WHYYY
I Want to cry out..
I want to die...
I feel miserable...
I feel so unstable...
What's up next?
Will this be the rest?
Why did this happen...
Why did i happen...

- Princess Shivangi Verma

35. " THAT GUY "

A young man with a heart full of love
For a girl, an angel from above
Though she may never know his heart
He wishes for her, a brand new start
He wants her to learn and to grow
To understand the world, to let it flow
He wants her to be strong and free
To live her life, wild and carefree
He watches from afar, with a heavy heart
As she struggles, torn apart
He longs to be by her side
To hold her hand, to be her guide
But he knows that his love, she may never see
And so he prays, for her, to be
Everything she was meant to be
To live a life of strength, wild and free
Though his love may never be returned
He'll always burn for her, forever yearned
For her happiness, he'll always strive
And in his heart, she'll always thrive
-Arun

36. THE ONE

Why do i feel the way i do?
I tried to stop, but the feelings grew!
I feel confusion and sadness...
I want to get away from this madness
"I was sitting next to you...
You kept your hand on mine...
I dazed into your eyes..."
I keep telling myself these lies!!!
When we talk and laugh...
Do you feel the same?
I feel like the efforts are all half..
Is is me? Is this a game?
Sliding when i see you approach..
Just so you could sit next to me..
And with a side eye i could see...
Thinking what all we could be..
Why can't you notice the one?
Trying to find..trying to run..
Spending time together is so fun..
But it's suffocating now..and I'm so done!
- princess shivangi verma

37. " IMAGINE "

A couple, hand in hand,
Together, they stand
Through the trials of life
They've found a love, without strife
They built a home, brick by brick
With love and laughter, it's a quick fix
For all their troubles, big or small
Together, they rise, and stand tall
They have a little girl, with pigtails and bows
Who brings them joy, and happiness flows
She runs around, with laughter and cheer
Their hearts are full, when she's near
They look back on their teenage dreams
Of a life together, it seems
It's all they ever wanted, and more
Their love, forever to soar
With each passing day, their love grows stronger
Together forever, they'll go on longer
Their lives, intertwined, forever entwined
In a love story, one of a kind
-Arun

38. TWO MONTHS TWELVE DAYS

two months twelve days
How much more...
Do i have to suffer?
I asked the almighty...
Tears dried up on my cheek..
Two months, twelve days dear...
She said with a smile...
You will know, the true colours
Not of butterflies or a flower..
But the people you call "yours"
Who give you pain and remorse...
Pretend to be angles,
But devils in disguise...
Break you from inside, and oh
Those endless sleepless nights..
You give them care,
They stab you in return...
They say they'll stay..
Instead they just run.

You've been turned away,
By every one of your own..
You've cried enough for those liars,
It's time for you to grow...
It has happened multiple times...
You too need to learn...
That no one, is trustworthy,
Be careful on every turn...
But don't you worry my love,
Every rose has to whither ,
Every sun has to set,
To your misery too,
There sure is an end.

-Princess shivangi verma

39. " THE CRUSH "

A young man with a heart full of fire
For a girl, he can't help but admire
She's the light in his dark days
But she's unaware of his secret ways
He watches her from afar
As she smiles and laughs, a shining star
But his love is unrequited, it seems
For she's in love with another, or so it seems
He wins and loses, every single day
As he watches her, in his own private play
He tries to hide his pain and despair
But it's there, etched in the lines of his face and hair
He tells himself, he's better off alone
But his love for her, has grown to be known
He knows deep down, it's a one-sided love
But he can't help it, it's as gentle as dove
He'll keep watching her, from a distance
Holding on to the thought of her existance
He'll keep his love for her, deep in his heart
And hope that one day, they'll never part.
-Arun

40. AN END TO IT

Is it jealousy

Or is it care?

Is it love..?

Or just a nightmare..

I wanna say it out loud..

But I'm a girl from the crowd..

Talking to me about her..

Whom do you really prefer?

We're so close..

Yet so far apart..

This is how it goes..

I need a new start...

We laugh as we talk..

Smile during our walk..

Yet it's all a mess..

And I'm in distress...

One day it'll end

Or it may change..

Or remain how it is..

Or I'll just pretend..

- Princess Shivangi Verma

41. " ROAD SIDE BOY "

A little boy, by the road he sat
With empty stomach, and a heart full of chat
He looked up at the sky so blue
Hoping someone, would see him too
His family, so poor, couldn't afford food
But he didn't let it bring him down, in his mood
He sat there with a smile on his face
A smile that could light up any place
He looked at the cars, going by
Hoping one would stop and give a try
To help him, to feed his family
With love, care and dignity
And then a man, with a heart of gold
Saw the little boy, young and bold
He stopped his car, and walked to him
And asked if he could help, with a grin
He took the little boy to a restaurant
And ordered him a meal, that was abundant
The little boy, with eyes shining bright
Ate the food, with pure delight

And the man, he looked on with pride
For he saw in the little boy, a great guide
A lesson for us all, to always smile
And to help others, every mile.
-Arun

42. NEVER WAKE UP AGAIN

It's 4 in the morning
I'm in my bed
Waiting for someone
Who'd come he said..
Why do i feel so..
Lost and alone..
Trying to love when
I need it the most..
Eyes feel so heavy..
But i cannot sleep ..
Something's so steady..
The way that i breathe.
I'll go to sleep now..
Will you just wait?
Will you be waiting..
Until I'm awake...
What if im sleeping..
And i get so scared..
I wake up screaming...
Screaming your name..

What if i find out..
That you are gone..
I'd sleep forever..
If I'm allowed...
Honey just come here,
I need you the most
Don't you disappear..
Hold me so close...
Until I wake up ..
Stay by my side..
And if i never..
I bid you goodbye...

- Princess Shivangi Verma
4:19 AM

43. " TILL THE END "

A heart once whole, now in shards,
Scattered upon the floor, like broken cards.
A love once beautiful, now torn apart,
Leaving me with a broken heart.
The pieces of my heart, sharp and cold,
A reminder of the love story, that's now old.
The silence of my tears, no one can hear,
As I drown in the pain, of this heartbreak, I fear.
The emptiness inside, a hollow ache,
A longing for comfort, I can't shake.
Memories of you, linger like a ghost,
Leaving me to suffer, at every cost.
I try to pick up the pieces, one by one,
But the task seems impossible, it's never done.
My heart is shattered, a mess to behold,
A love, that once was, now forever told.
I'll keep the shards, as a reminder,
Of the love, that once was, a sinder.
And though my heart may never mend,
I'll hold on to the love, till the very end..
-Arun

44. LOOSING MYSELF

Oo, when was that day..?
When the good days ended..
The sky turned to ashes...
And turned the void grey...
The only way forward..
Is down stairs..
None of the efforts-
Take me up but push me down..
I keep waiting with a frown..

And i lost ..
to growing demons,
In my head..
Don't know what to do..like i said..
It's hard not to look ahead..
Loosing myself,
Is worse than loosing others..
But if you ask what made me this way..
When the people i love, left, i would say..
Memories, gifts or empty words..
Nothing makes me feel alright..
Is Lying to my face so easy?

You just push me back everytime..
If i look behind i see dark past..
Where i stand now is not so bright..
Ahead of me lies unknown start..
Where do I go..? It's all a fight.
-princess shivangi verma

45. '" HEART OF A POOR BOY "

My heart was once full of love and light
But now it's dark and filled with plight
I was a poor boy, from a humble home
And she was my everything, my guiding light, my dome
But fate had other plans, for her and I
And she was taken away, with a love that wasn't mine
My world crumbled, my heart in pieces
As she wed another, my love decreases
I wander now, with a heavy heart
Thinking of all the moments we'll never start
I'll always love her, and that will never change
But my poor heart will forever be estranged
I'll hold on to the memories, that we shared
And the love that once, we dared
But now she's gone, and I'm alone
A poor boy, without a home.
-Arun

46. LOVE YOU FOREVER

I love you so much..
And I will keep loving you...
Till the day I inhale my last breath...
When your away..
I feel so incomplete..
Which is kind of amusing..
Cause you never were near, Yet..
I feel as if I'm the luckiest person alive..
To be in love with someone like you..
Even if it's a one sided emotion..
You make every sorrow go away,
Just by your presence..
I love you to the square of infinity..
everytime I close my eyes..
it's your slight smiling face that I see,
That gets me all happy and pink..
You make me feel okay!
Without even realising it!
You are someone, I never want to loose,

Even if that means I can't have you..
All to myself..your heart is someone else's,
Your heart won't ever be mine..
We never will be a love story..
But the love that I hold for you,
Is enough to my heart and soul..
You don't feel the same about me,
And that's okay honey..
I will still love you..
FOREVER...like i do..<3
-Princess Shivangi Verma

47. " MY VAENTINE "

My love, my heart, my shining star
You light up my life, from near and far
In your eyes, I see my future
With you by my side, my heart feels pure
Your smile, it warms my soul
With you, I am whole
With every touch, every kiss
I am lost in your bliss
You are my everything, my reason to live
With you, my love will never wilt or shrivel
I'll love you forever, till the end of time
You are my partner, my confidant, my one and only
Valentine.
You are my sun on a gloomy day
My north star, that guides me on my way
With you, my heart sings a sweet melody
You make my life complete, my love for you will always be
I promise to love you, till the end of time
To be your partner, your confidant,
your everything, my gorgeous, my Valentine.
-Arun

48. LOVED TOO DIFFERENTLY

I guess love is just like rain,
It falls on us magically,
But leaves puddles for us to hold-
On to it's beauty..
Yes, she'll probably always love him,
From here to many others incarnations..
The only difference was..
One couldnt Love..
And the other one couldn't stop..
And they were on the same page..
Not knowing that it was the last one...
As time passed by, she realised,
How the word forever-
Is for the memories..
Not people...
They loved too differently...
she saw the beauty of infinite inside him..
Until he showed her...
Finite is just ethereal...

But no matter what happens,
Or how much it rains ..
The puddle shall dry up..
By the sun that shines bright...
Still remembering the infinite..
-Princess Shivangi Verma

49. " FATHER'S LOVE "

I remember the days when I was young,
My father's love for me was never undone.
He would hold me close, give me kisses and hugs,
And take me out for ice cream, and to play at the parks.
But now as I've grown, things have changed,
My father's love has been rearranged.
He's become strict, and distant too,
And I long for the love he used to do.
I miss those days, when he would play,
And we would laugh, and chase the day.
But now it's different, he's not the same,
And it's like I've lost a part of my game.
I understand that he wants the best for me,
But it hurts to see his love set free.
I wish I could go back in time,
To those days, when everything was fine.
I'll always cherish the memories we've made,
And the love that once, never fade.
But now, I long for his embrace,
And to feel his love, in a special place.

But as I look back on all the years
I remember the joy, the laughter, the cheers
Though the love may have changed, it's still there
Etched in my heart, forever to compare
For a father's love is never truly gone
It's the foundation upon which I stand strong
And though the shape of it may shift and bend
It's a love that will never, truly end.
-Arun

50. CONTROL

What do you think love is?
Is it care maybe?
Or when they call you baby?
Or when their smile makes you crazy!
When you feel protected,
The way that they get jealous..
When they always want you,
How they say their love is true..
They get really mad..
When you are at fault..
They say it's their care..
But their thoughts are at halt..
Anger, trust and jealousy..
All your actions are bound..
Your efforts seem limitless..
You theirs are not found..
Your always in a fight or flight,
Remember their death stare?
They make you try with all your might..
You ask - It's LOVE, they declare.
Maybe love needs efforts you think..
You keep up with their lows and highs..

Your never enough..your on the brink..
You climb, when your afraid of heights..
Controlling you makes them feel fine..
They cannot control who they are..
They cage you up and call you 'mine'
All this does is leave a scar..
Your souls helps them heal..
Heal what they feel inside..
But they are breaking you now..
And you don't realise it in time..
You are exhausted.. Never enough..
Always feeling empty inside..
Keeping up with this is so tough.
It's making your inner child die..
But you keep going back...
Forgetting everything..
How would you not though..?
They hold you by an invisible string..
I know that it seems rough..
You look up at the sky..
I wish the haze clears up,
And you soon realise..
Toxic love - is not love
Their issues don't justify..
What they do to you,
How they hold you down,
Make you feel like a clown,

Let go, what your trying to hold..
Stop doing what you have been told.
Love is like a soothing river ...
Flowing effortlessly along..
Love makes you smile..
Love makes you strong..
You are not their vent,
but their safe place.
You help one another throught the days,
You grow together and touch the sky,
Even when you are afraid of heights.
-Princess Shivangi Verma

51. " SOMETHING HIDDEN "

In solitude, I oft' do sit
lost in thought, alone, I do quiver
overwhelmed by emotions, my eyes flit
visions of a future, I forever deliver
endless days and restless nights
my future, a mystery, I can't deny
only i knows what i wants in sight
unceasingly striving, i'll give it a try
many times i feel the pain
and the world thinks , i will never attain
To the world, i'll show my worth, a gain
A life of love, where they'll always be
vibrant petals dance in the breeze, a symphony of colours
that never cease.
in mountains high, they'll find their peace
Her love, a light that shines so bright
With her by my side, i'll see it through
And build a future, that's pure and white
- Arun

52. WHO WE ARE ?

You are a plant!
Yes you are!
Why you may ask,
Let's look at your heart..
If a seed doesn't grow,
The flower doesn't bloom,
Would you blame the seed?
Or is it absence of monsoon..?
How can you expect a plant-
To pop out happy and fine,
Without watering the soil..
Without a little sunshine..?
Would you blame the seed..?
Or the environment around..
That won't let it grow..
Like the infertile ground..
You are a seed indeed,
The seed feels small and needless..
Darkness surrounds when in the ground..
And all that weight of responsibilities!
But what it doesn't know,
It has been sown in deep,

What it will grow to be,
This is making it stronger, it'll see!
Yes, that effects what surrounds,
To no weight the seed is bound,
But every flower needs a bud before,
And the beauty is held deep in store!
The people, the place the negativity,
That builds up on your mind,
Turns you into someone your not,
Among all this you need to find..
Your not lost, you just closed your eyes,
Open them up and see the bright!
The day begins new, after every night!
Open up, try again, there's no fright!
You'll bloom once you find,
What I call - your sunshine!
The seed isn't worthless at all,
Everything always starts small.
So calm down and say along
I'm a plant, and I'll grow oo so tall!
Nothing pulls me back or slows me down,
My efforts will make me come out the ground.
-Princess Shivangi Verma

I never really knew you
you were just another friend
But when I got to know you
I let my heart unbend
I couldn't help past memories
That would only make me cry
I had to forget my first love
And give another try
So I've fallen in love with you
And I'll never let you go
I love you more than anyone
I just had to let you know
My feelings for you will never change
Just know my feelings are true
Just remember this one thing
I will always be there for you

"Our Mini Infinity: A Journey Through Emotions"

Discover a world of emotions with "Our Mini Infinity: A Journey Through Emotions", a new poetry book written by two young, talented authors, Arun kumar and Princess Shivangi Verma. This collection of poems takes you on a roller coaster of feelings, exploring love, pain, butterflies, confusion, loneliness and joy.

Every word in this book holds a backstory, written at a time when emotions were at their peak, the authors used their writing as a way to cope with and express their feelings. This book is a testament to the power of words, and the impact they can have on our lives.

The authors invite you to join them in their world of mini infinity, where you can find solace and comfort in the shared experiences of others. The poems in this book are relatable, raw and honest, and will make you feel every emotion that you've ever experienced.

Follow the journey on Instagram at @ourminiinfinity01, where you can stay updated on all things "Our Mini Infinity". The authors, Arun kumar (@dude_arun427) and Princess Shivangi Verma (@princess_shivangi_verma) are active on the platform, sharing their thoughts and experiences as poets, and providing a behind-the-scenes look at the creative process.